THE DEBT DRAGON

Created by Barry Elwonger
Published by Little Ledger Press
'Big lessons from little stories.'

www.LittleLedgerPress.com

Little Ledger Press

ISBN 979-8-9987478-1-6
First Edition

Brooke loved her library, a castle
filled with books and magic.
Every day, she read stories with
the villagers. They laughed,
learned, and dreamed together.

One day, a big storm swept through the village. Wind howled, rain poured, and the roof of the library was badly damaged. Water dripped through the cracks, ruining most of the books.

Brooke felt sad as she saw the soggy, ruined pages.

"I need coins to fix the roof and buy new books," she said.

Brooke worked hard to collect coins,
but despite her effort, it wasn't enough
for the repairs.

As she stared up at the damage, she
remembered an old story about the
Debt Dragon, a creature made entirely
of gold coins!

The dragon lends coins to anyone who asks, Brooke recalled.

But there's a catch: if you don't pay him back on time, he grows bigger, stronger, and greedier.

Despite the warning, Brooke thought the Debt Dragon sounded kind and generous.

"I'll borrow just enough coins to fix the roof
and buy new books," she said.
"I'll pay him back later when I have more money."

Brooke traveled to the
dragon's cave, where
piles of coins glittered in
the dim light.
The Debt Dragon smiled
as Brooke approached.

"You may borrow my coins," he said.
"But remember, you must pay me back with interest.
If you don't pay me on time, you'll owe me even more."

Broke signed the contract, took a bag of coins, and thanked the dragon. She left with a smile, thinking everything would be fine.

With the borrowed coins, Brooke
fixed the roof and bought new books.
The library was as good as new!
The villagers were happy, and
Brooke felt proud.

As time went on, Brooke forgot about the Debt Dragon and the contract. She was too busy enjoying the new library to think about paying him back.

Meanwhile, the Debt Dragon hadn't forgotten. From his cave, he watched Brooke and the villagers laughing and reading. He grumbled to himself, "They borrowed my coins, but they're not paying me back. Now I'll make them pay, with more interest!"

As the dragon grew greedier, he piled
on more coins and more debt for Brooke.

The next day, the dragon sent a letter to Brooke. It read:

To Brooke

YOU OWE ME
MORE COINS
THAN YOU
BORROWED,
PAY ME BACK
NOW, OR, I'LL
TAKE EVERYTHING
YOU HAVE!

DEBT

Brooke was shocked when she read the letter. "How did this happen?" she cried. "I only borrowed one bag of coins, but now I owe ten! I can't pay him back. What will I do?"

Brooke gathered the villagers and told them everything. "I made a mistake," she admitted. "I borrowed money from the Debt Dragon, and I didn't pay him back. Now he wants more coins than I have. If I don't pay him back, he'll take everything, including our library!"

The villagers listened carefully.
Then one of them said,
"We will help you, Brooke.
We will work hard and earn
coins.
Together, we can pay him
back."

Brooke and the villagers got to work right away. They used their magic and skills to earn coins as quickly as they could.
Every day, they paid the dragon something, but at first, they could only pay a little.

The Debt Dragon stayed the same size, thinking, "As long as they keep paying only the minimum, I'll stay big and strong."

But Brooke and the villagers didn't just pay the minimum. They worked harder, earned extra coins, and gave the dragon more each day.

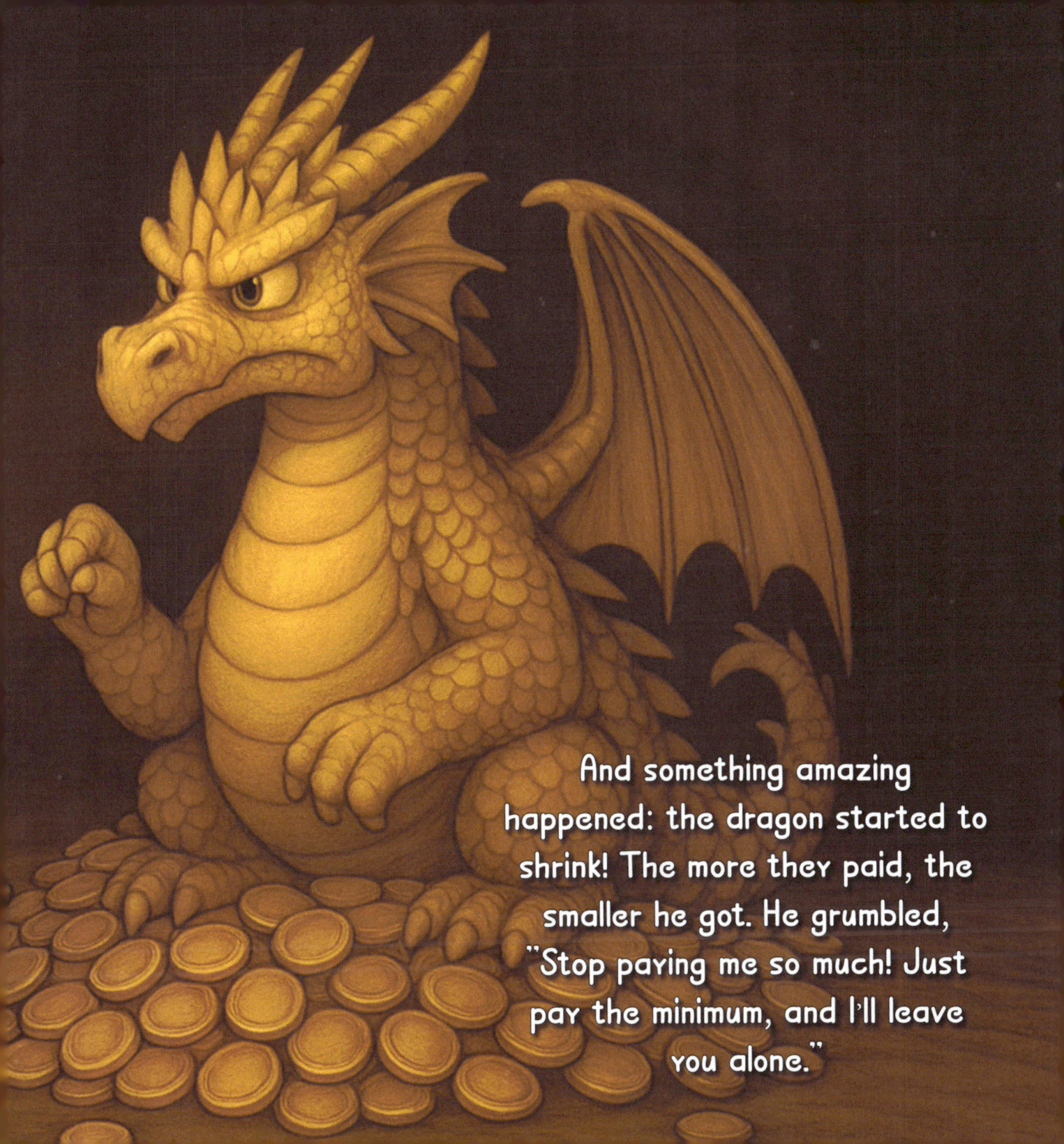

And something amazing happened: the dragon started to shrink! The more they paid, the smaller he got. He grumbled, "Stop paying me so much! Just pay the minimum, and I'll leave you alone."

Brooke and the villagers refused to stop.
"No," they said firmly. "We won't pay the minimum.
We'll pay you back in full. We don't want to owe
you anything at all!"

Day after day, they worked and paid, until one day the Debt Dragon was gone. They had paid him back completely and were free from his grasp.

Brooke and the villagers stood outside the library, smiling with relief. They were proud of what they had achieved.
They had worked hard, paid off their debt, and saved their library.

"We did it," Brooke said. "We paid the Debt Dragon. We learned our lesson, and we won't borrow from him again."

To make sure they were never in trouble again, the villagers built a coffer of savings. They put aside a little bit of what they earned every day.

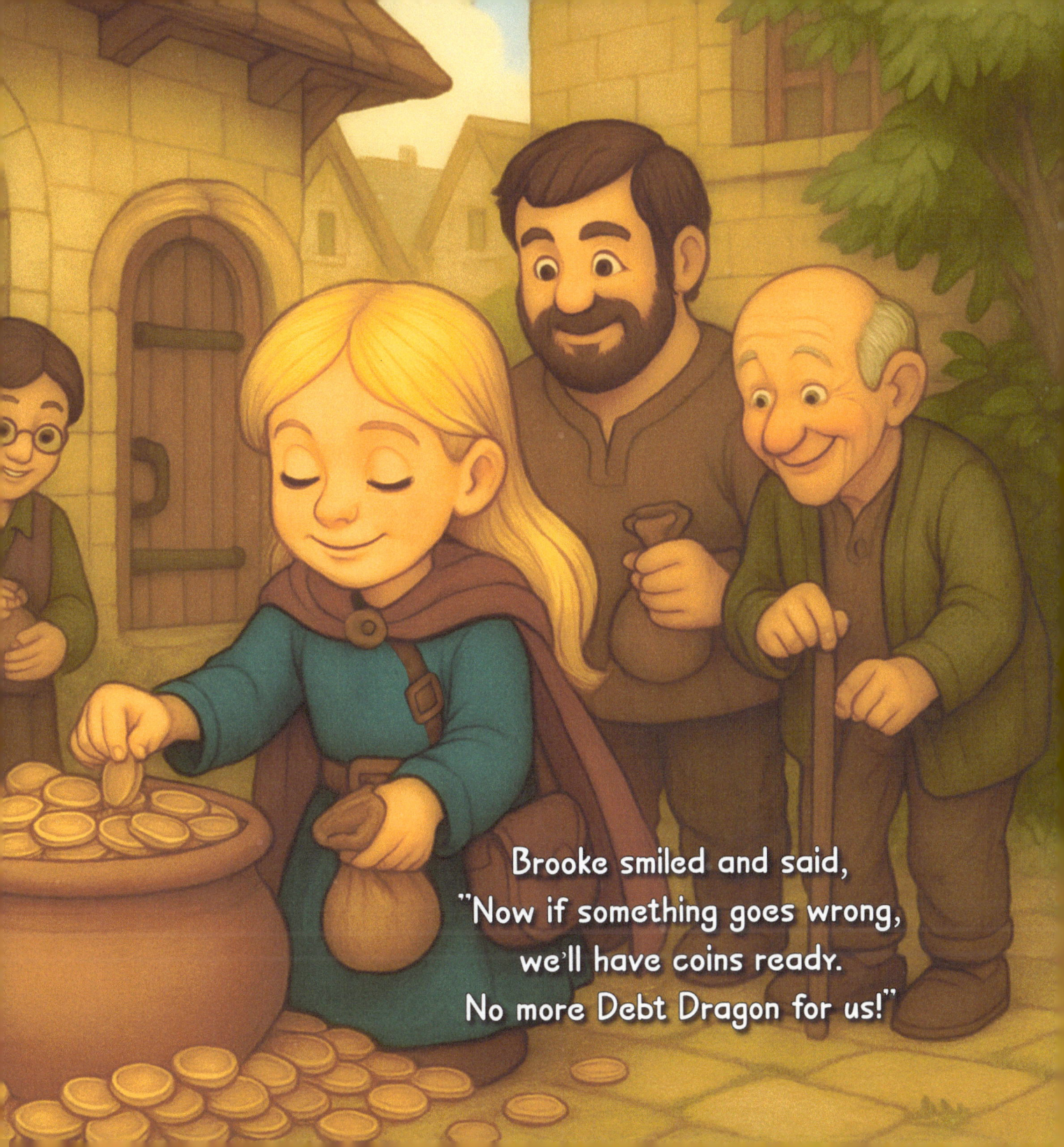

Brooke smiled and said,
"Now if something goes wrong,
we'll have coins ready.
No more Debt Dragon for us!"

From that day on, Brooke and the villagers enjoyed their library without worry, knowing they had learned how to save for the future.

More Adventures Await!

Explore other adventures in the Brooke Will Not Be Broke Series:

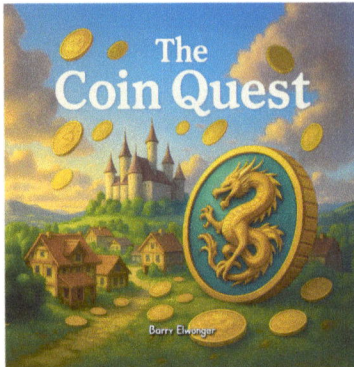

The Coin Quest — Barry Elwonger

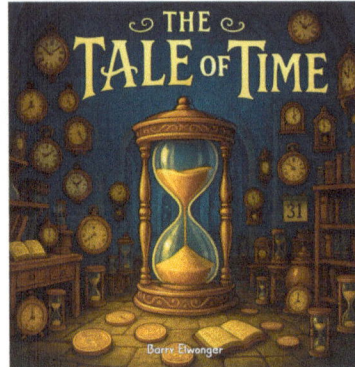

The Tale of Time — Barry Elwonger

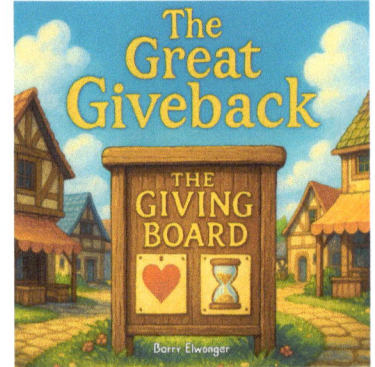

The Great Giveback — The Giving Board — Barry Elwonger

All proceeds from this book series go directly to support Brooke and Blake's college funds. Thanks for helping young readers dream big - and plan smart.

Little Ledger Press

For more books, resources, and free downloads visit:

www.LittleLedgerPress.com

www.ingramcontent.com/pod-product-compliance
Lightning Source LLC
Chambersburg PA
CBHW050912210326
41597CB00002B/97

* 9 7 9 8 9 9 8 7 4 7 8 1 6 *